JOINTS AND GLANDS EXERCISES

AS TAUGHT BY SRI SWAMI RAMA OF THE HIMALAYAS

Edited by Rudolph M. Ballentine Jr., M.D.

Illustrations by Rashmi

Published by
THE HIMALAYAN INTERNATIONAL INSTITUTE
OF YOGA SCIENCE AND PHILOSOPHY

ISBN 0-89389-030-8

First Edition,	1973
Second Edition,	1974
Third Edition	1976
Fourth Edition	1977
Fifth Edition	1978
Second Printing	1978

Himalayan International Institute
of Yoga Science and Philosophy
Honesdale, Pennsylvania 18431

FOREWORD

If you watch a cat or a dog when it wakes up, you'll see that it goes through an elaborate process of stretching. One leg, for example, is put far back and the body is stretched away from it as much as possible. You may do something similar when you climb out of bed in the morning. Putting your arms high above your head and stretching up to the tips of your toes seems like a natural part of coming out of sleep.

But why do you do this? Mostly because it feels good. You may not think about it much but it seems to get the body back into comfortable, working order. It re-coordinates the system and makes you feel more "alive."

At first glance it seems like an insignificant thing, this luxurious morning stretch. But there is a very important principle underlying it. Researchers have begun to discover the importance of what they call the "body image." One's mental picture of himself determines to a great extent which parts of his body he uses actively and which parts he sort of "forgets." A person whose awareness centers around his face and chest, for instance, may have a pleasant expression and dress neatly, while he tends to ignore his spine and the back part of his body. His basic posture suffers as a result. He will, without being particularly conscious of it, allow his upper spine to slump into a hunchback position. After years of habitually sitting and standing this way the back becomes "frozen." In a sense it doesn't get the "energy" that is necessary to keep it flexible and healthy. Calcifications and other disorders of the spine are likely to follow.

We might say, then, that when a person "forgets" a part of his body, it suffers serious consequences. When it is not properly positioned, movements around it are not properly regulated. One set of muscles becomes weak from disuse, another overdeveloped from the effort to maintain an off-balance position.

Yoga postures are designed to break up such bad habits by systematically exercising different parts of the body in a gentle, pleasant way. One gradually brings back into his awareness muscles and joints that have over the years become "forgotten." Muscles which had become weak are gradually and gently strengthened so that the body can once more be held in a comfortable and natural position. Posture is improved so that energy may begin to flow again in a natural, exhilarating way.

In the science and philosophy of Yoga the basis for these exercises is outlined in great detail. The physical body is said to be only one of several "bodies" which make up the human system. The way we picture ourselves, our mental image of our "shape" is part of what is called the "mental body." Besides this and the physical body which we can see and touch, there is an intermediate level which has to do with the energy that activates our muscles, glands and so forth. We might compare it to the electricity that makes a motor run. The energy must flow through the right channels and enter the right circuits if the machine is to function smoothly. The energy, the physical body and the mental "body image" interact in an intricate way. But one need not trouble himself with the theory in order to enjoy the benefits of yogic exercises.

In fact, it is not even necessary to struggle with the complex and difficult poses which are usually described in Yoga manuals. Actually, they only become really useful once the body has begun to move back towards a natural balance. Meanwhile, the joint and gland exercises are a set of simple, pleasant "stretches" which can be used with great benefit by almost anyone regardless of how badly he is "out of shape." By increasing the circulation to different parts of the body and by restoring a natural, flowing "body image" in the mind, a harmonious feeling of energy throughout the system can be re-established. This means that all the structures, including the "joints and glands" benefit. One beneficial effect of the exercises accentuates another. The results can be very gratifying. It comes as a surprise to many people that they can feel better each day instead of worse!

It should be kept in mind that these are "stretches." They should be as pleasant and enjoyable as that first exuberant stretch that comes spontaneously on stepping out of bed. Done slowly, gently and with enjoyment they can be most effective.

Rudolph M. Ballentine Jr., M.D.
Glenview, Illinois

CONTENTS

INTRODUCTION

The practice of joint and gland exercises can be used to prepare the student for the practice of Hatha Yoga or they can be used simply for their own intrinsic value. These exercises have been studied and investigated for nearly ten years in the United States and have proved to be most beneficial. It is recommended that all students practice them for one month before beginning Hatha postures.

The exercises are arranged in a very systematic way: the student starts at the top of his head and continues downward, exercising and massaging almost all of the joints and glands. Each part of the body receives a good supply of blood. The muscles are made supple, more flexible, the joints and the glands are toned and made to function properly.

These exercises are highly recommended for persons suffering from arthritis, rheumatism or stiffness. They are a safe way of getting started on the path to better health. They lead one toward perfection of the body and calmness of the mind. When the body becomes calm and relaxed, the mind becomes peaceful.

General Instructions:

Practice daily, be regular, always move slowly with concentration on your movements. Try to be aware of the breath at all times and unless otherwise specified, keep the breath even. Repeat all exercises three times but avoid going beyond your capacity. When you feel strain, stop and relax, then proceed more gently.

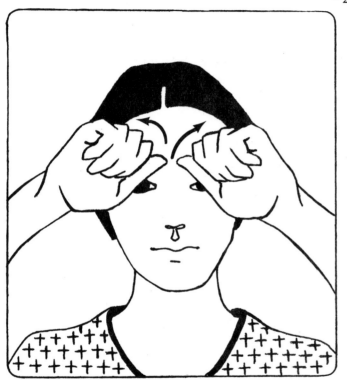

Figure 1

FACE

FOREHEAD & SINUS MASSAGE

1. Sit in a comfortable, crosslegged position with the head, neck and trunk straight. Make a loose fist with both hands, the thumb against the forehead between the two eyebrows. (Figure 1)

   Begin to massage the forehead with the thumbs by working up and out with a stroking motion. Follow the bony structure around the eyes and continue out across the temples.

2. Next, place the side of the thumbs on the face just below the eyes and next to the nose, one on each side. (Figure 2)

Make the same motions moving outwards across the face and temples.

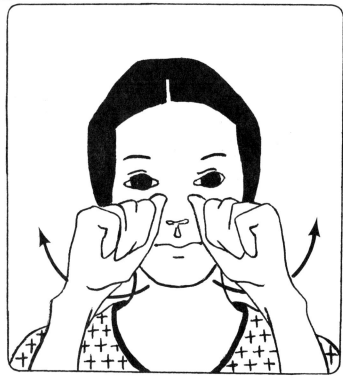

Figure 2

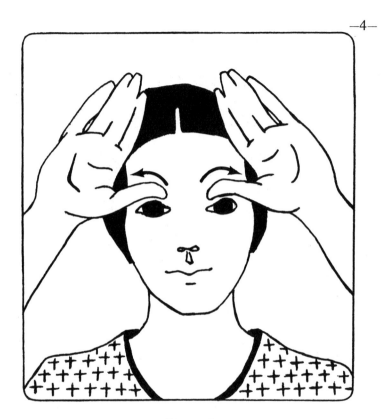

Figure 3

3. Open the hands. Using the undersides of the thumbs, gently slide the thumbs across the upper rim of the eye sockets towards the temples. (Figure 3)

4. Likewise, massage with the index fingers the lower rim of the eye sockets towards the temples. (Figure 4)

All of these movements begin at the center of the face and move outwards. This pushes all the tension off the face, forehead, and temples and smooths away any wrinkles on the forehead or crows-feet at the eye edges. This massage may help break up and loosen any mucus obstructions in the nasal sinuses.

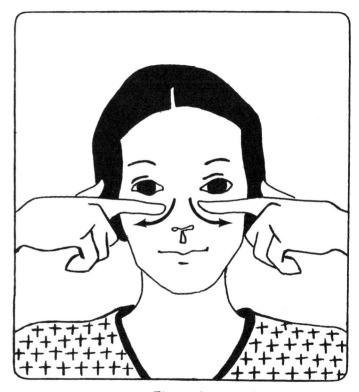

Figure 4

Figure 5

SCALP & FOREHEAD

1. Keeping the eyes focused straight forward and the head stationary, raise the eyebrows slowly without any jerks or quick movements as high as you can. Create tension and wrinkles on the forehead. (Figure 5)

Slowly lower the eyebrows, releasing the tension from the forehead.

HALF FACE SQUINT

1. Place the right hand gently against the right side of the face and squint slowly and then relax the entire left side, keeping the right side completely relaxed. (Figure 6)

   Repeat squint on right side. The division between the muscles tensed and those remaining relaxed should be very definite. One eye should be tense and the other relaxed. Half the mouth should be tense and half relaxed. In the beginning the hand is used only as an aid to assist in learning how to isolate the muscles. After some time the hand should not be used.

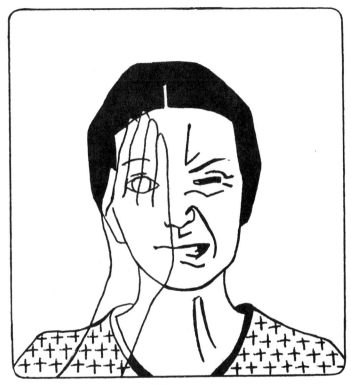

Figure 6

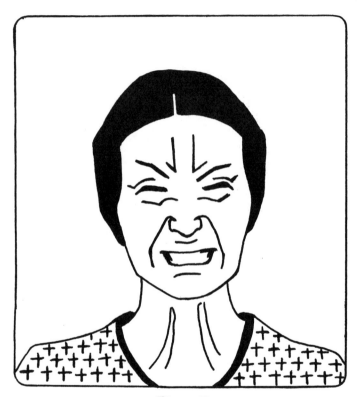

Figure 7

FULL FACE SQUINT

1. Squint and tense all the muscles of the face pulling them to the tip of the nose, as if the nose was the center of gravity. (Figure 7) Relax.

EYES

Keep the head stationary and facial muscles relaxed in the following eye exercises. For several seconds after each variation, relax the eyes by gently closing them. All eye exercises are done three times in each direction or to your capacity.

1. Start with the eyes straight forward, then slowly turn the eyes to the left as far as possible. Feel the stretch in the eye muscles, slowly come back to the forward position. (Figure 8)

   Look to the right in the same manner and again return to the forward position. Always balance what you do on one side by doing the same thing to the opposite side, holding for the same length of time in each direction.

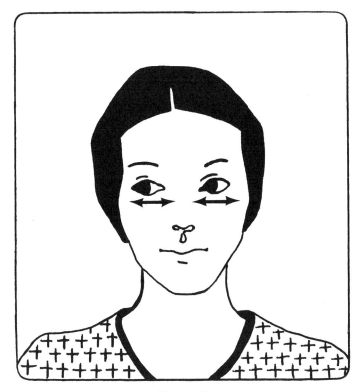

Figure 8

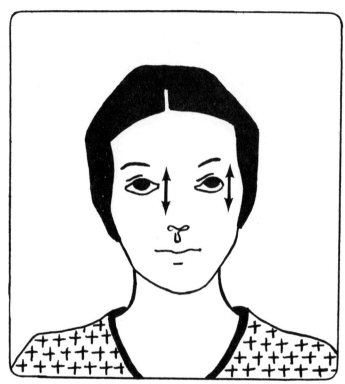

Figure 9

2. Turn the eyes towards the ceiling, then bring the eyes back to the forward position. Look down and again bring the eyes back to the forward position, then relax by closing the eyes. (Figure 9)

Figure 10

3. Look to the upper left hand corner. Bring the eyes back to the forward position. Look to the lower right hand corner and return the eyes to the forward position.

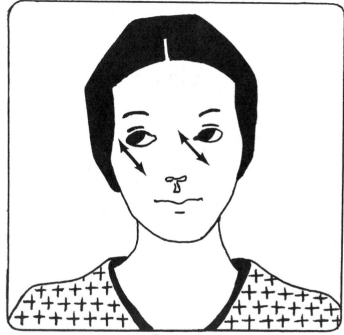

Figure 11

4. Look to the lower left hand corner, return to the forward position. Look towards the upper right hand corner and again back to forward position. Relax by closing eyes.

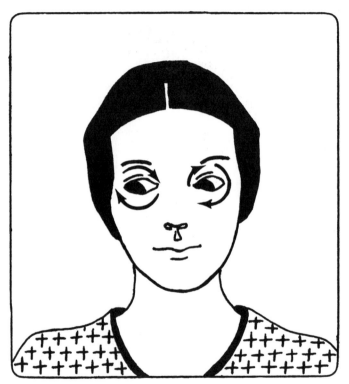

Figure 12

5. First look downwards, then start the eyes rolling in a clockwise motion making a complete circle.

6. Reverse the process moving the eyes in a counter-clockwise direction. The movements should be slow and free from jerks. Relax by closing eyes. (Figure 12)

7. Close the eyes and squeeze the lids together very tightly for five seconds. Now blink the eyelids as rapidly as you can. Relax by closing the eyes gently so that the eyelids barely touch.

MOUTH

1. Grit the teeth and stretch the lips in a wide grin. The muscles and the tendons of the neck should protrude like cords stretching from underneath your chin to your shoulder. (Figure 13) Gently relax.

2. Open the mouth, pull the lips tightly over the teeth so that they do not show. Drop the chin as far as possible and stretch the mouth into the shape of an "O." The movement is similar to a yawn. Keeping the mouth as far open as possible, curl the upper lip back as if to touch the nose and the lower lip down as if to touch the chin. Close the mouth, now curl both lips upwards trying to touch the tip of the nose. Relax completely.

Figure 13

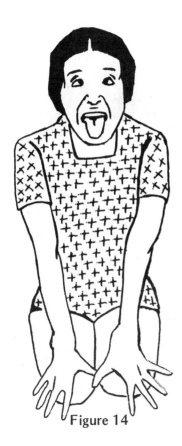

Figure 14

LION

This exercise involves the whole body but the attention is focused on the mouth and throat. Sit in a kneeling position (buttocks upon the heels) with the head, neck and trunk straight. Place the hands on the knees, palms down. Exhale and all in the same movement, lift slightly off the heels leaning forward. Straighten the arms, spread the fingers apart, keeping the hands on the knees. Open the mouth as wide as possible and thrust the tongue out and down, trying to touch the chin. Gaze at the point between the two eyebrows. The whole body should be tensed. Retain the breath while holding this position. (Figure 14) Relax with an inhalation and sit back on the heels. The lion is also an *asana*. It is good for sore throats, as circulation is increased to the throat area. It improves foul breath and clarity of speech. It also is said to strengthen intellectual faculties.

FACE MASSAGE

Using the heel of the hand, massage the entire face, following the bony structure of the forehead, eyes, cheeks and mouth, smoothing the muscles and the skin. (Figure 15)

This massage removes any tension left in the facial muscles from doing the previous exercises, and it smooths out wrinkles resulting from continuous tension in the face.

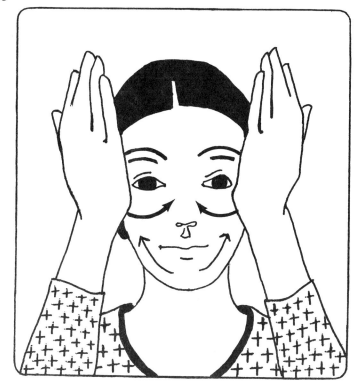

Figure 15

Figure 16

NECK

The starting position for all the neck exercises is the same; sit with the head, neck and trunk straight, facing forward. The shoulders should not move in any of the neck exercises, only the neck and the head should move.

FORWARD & BACKWARD BEND

1. Exhale slowly bringing the head forward, taking the chin towards the chest. Feel the stretch of the muscles in the back of the neck. Inhale slowly, lifting the head up and back stretching the muscles of the front of the neck. With an exhalation, slowly return to the forward position. (Figure 16)

CHIN OVER SHOULDER

2. With an exhalation, turn the head as far to the left as possible and try to bring the chin in line with the shoulder. Inhale and bring the head back to the forward position. Repeat in the same manner on the right side. (Figure 17)

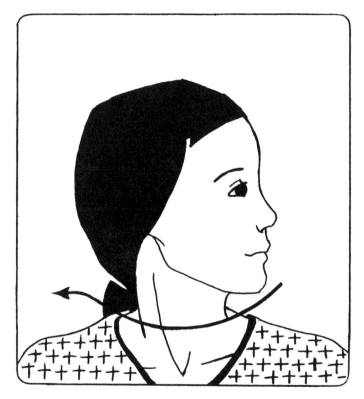

Figure 17

Figure 18

EAR TO SHOULDER

3. With an exhalation, bring the left ear towards the left shoulder. Inhale, come back to the center. Exhaling, bring the right ear towards the right shoulder. Again inhale, come back to the center and relax. Only the head and neck should move. The shoulder should not be raised to meet the ear. (Figure 18)

TURTLE

4. Keeping the shoulders stationary, exhale and thrust the chin and head as far forward as possible, keeping the mouth closed and the teeth together. Inhaling, slowly come back to the center, then moving the head back, tuck the chin into the neck, forcing an extreme double chin. (Figure 19) Exhale and relax returning to the center position.

Figure 19

Figure 20

NECK ROLLS

5. Lower the chin to the chest and slowly begin to rotate the head in a clockwise direction. Inhale while lifting the head up and back and exhale when bringing it forward and down. Reverse and rotate the same number of times in the opposite, counter-clockwise direction. The head, neck and body should be relaxed, allowing the head to rotate freely and loosely. (Figure 20)

SHOULDERS

LIFTS

1. These are exercises on tension and relaxation. Stand firm with the arms hanging loosely at the sides. Without moving the head, slowly tense, lift the left shoulder up trying to touch it to the left ear. All at once, relax and drop the shoulder. Do the same for the right shoulder, then very slowly raise both shoulders as high as you can. Hold for a few seconds and then very slowly relax the shoulder completely. (Figure 21)

Figure 21

Figure 22

ROTATIONS

2. Stand with the arms hanging loosely at the sides. Begin to rotate the left shoulder in a complete circle, first moving it forward and in towards the center of the chest. Then, move it up towards the ear and back, trying to touch the shoulder-blade to the spine, and then down back into the starting position. Rotate three times in this direction and then reverse and rotate three times in the opposite direction. Do the same for the right shoulder and then with both shoulders together. (Figure 22) Relax.

ROTATION WITH HANDS
TO SHOULDER

Figure 23a

3a. Stand firm with the arms extended out in front of you at chest height. Turn the palms up. The shoulders should be relaxed. Begin to rotate the shoulders. First forward and up. Raise the arms high over the head with the palms facing back, and then back and down. Relax the arms at the elbows and the fingers descend towards and touch the shoulders. (Figure 23a)

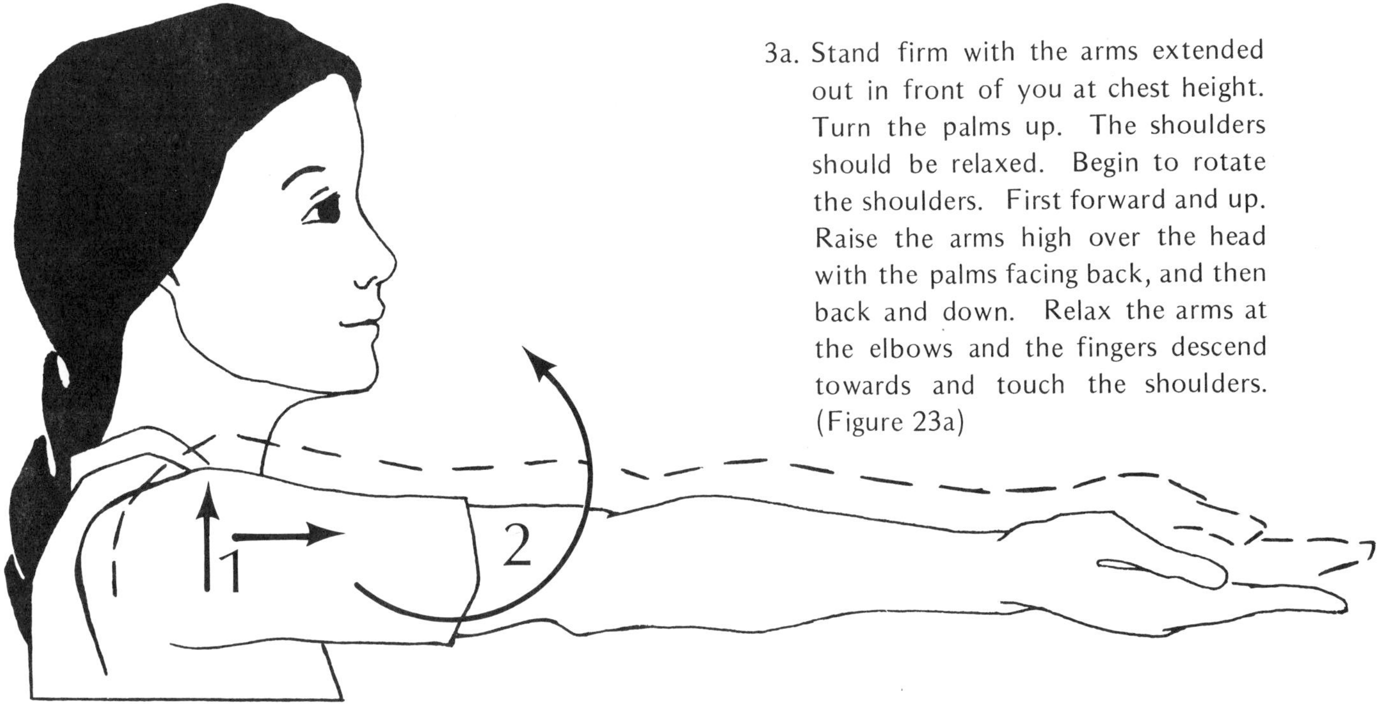

ROTATION WITH HANDS TO SHOULDER

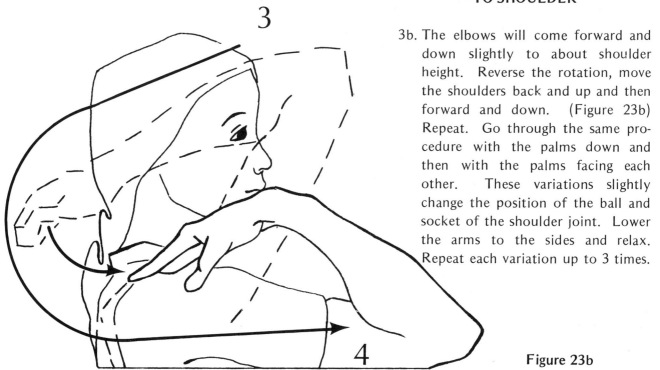

3

4

3b. The elbows will come forward and down slightly to about shoulder height. Reverse the rotation, move the shoulders back and up and then forward and down. (Figure 23b) Repeat. Go through the same procedure with the palms down and then with the palms facing each other. These variations slightly change the position of the ball and socket of the shoulder joint. Lower the arms to the sides and relax. Repeat each variation up to 3 times.

Figure 23b

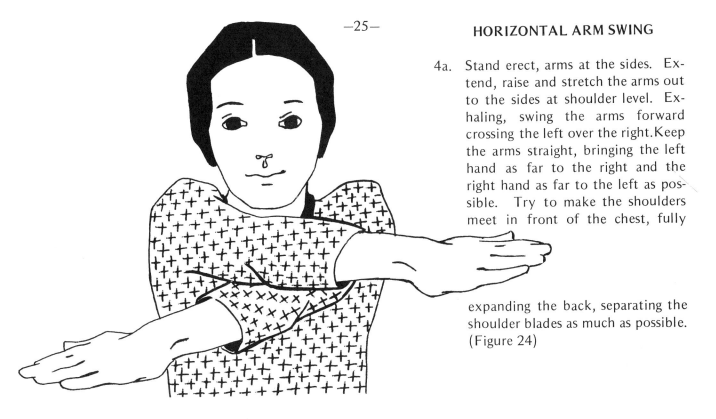

Figure 24

HORIZONTAL ARM SWING

4a. Stand erect, arms at the sides. Extend, raise and stretch the arms out to the sides at shoulder level. Exhaling, swing the arms forward crossing the left over the right. Keep the arms straight, bringing the left hand as far to the right and the right hand as far to the left as possible. Try to make the shoulders meet in front of the chest, fully expanding the back, separating the shoulder blades as much as possible. (Figure 24)

HORIZONTAL ARM SWING

4b. Inhaling, swing the arms back out to the sides and behind, expanding the chest and bringing the shoulder-blades close together. (Figure 25) Do this three times in one continuous motion, then repeat three times with the right arm over the left or alternate on each swing.

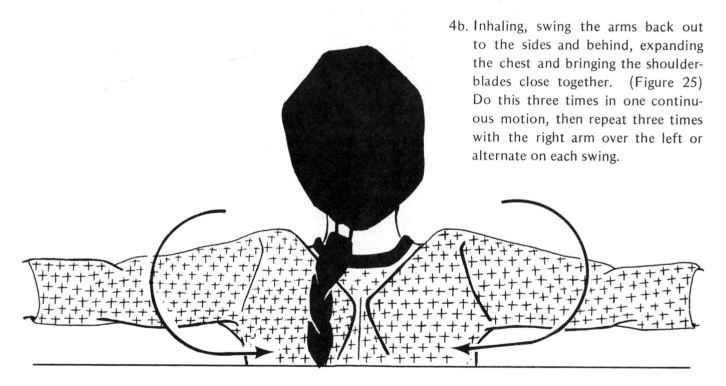

Figure 25

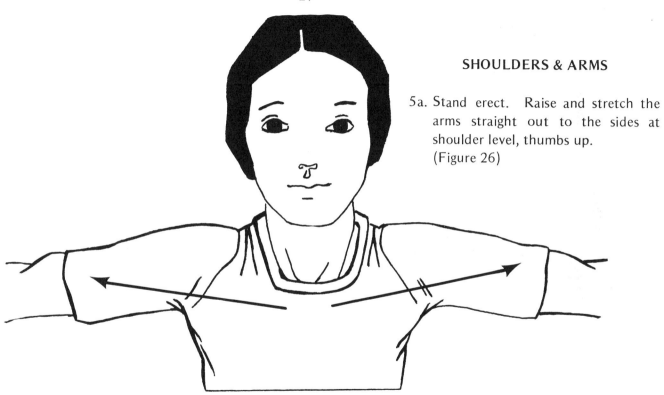

SHOULDERS & ARMS

5a. Stand erect. Raise and stretch the arms straight out to the sides at shoulder level, thumbs up. (Figure 26)

Figure 26

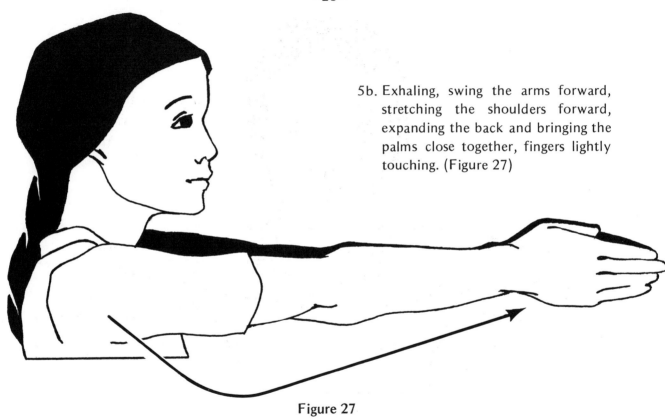

5b. Exhaling, swing the arms forward, stretching the shoulders forward, expanding the back and bringing the palms close together, fingers lightly touching. (Figure 27)

Figure 27

5c. Inhale, bringing the palms to the chest and expand the chest, elbows bent. The elbows remain at shoulder level. (Figure 28)

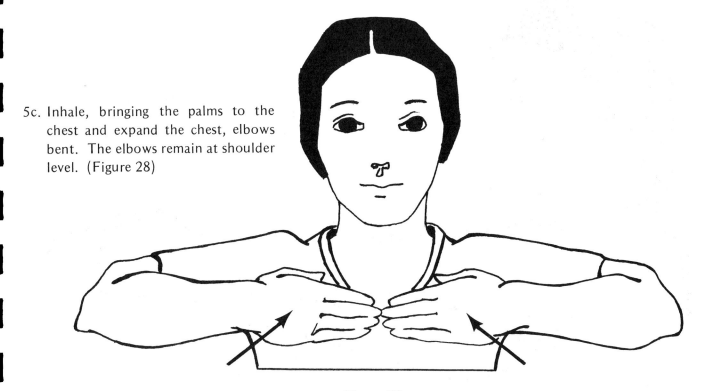

Figure 28

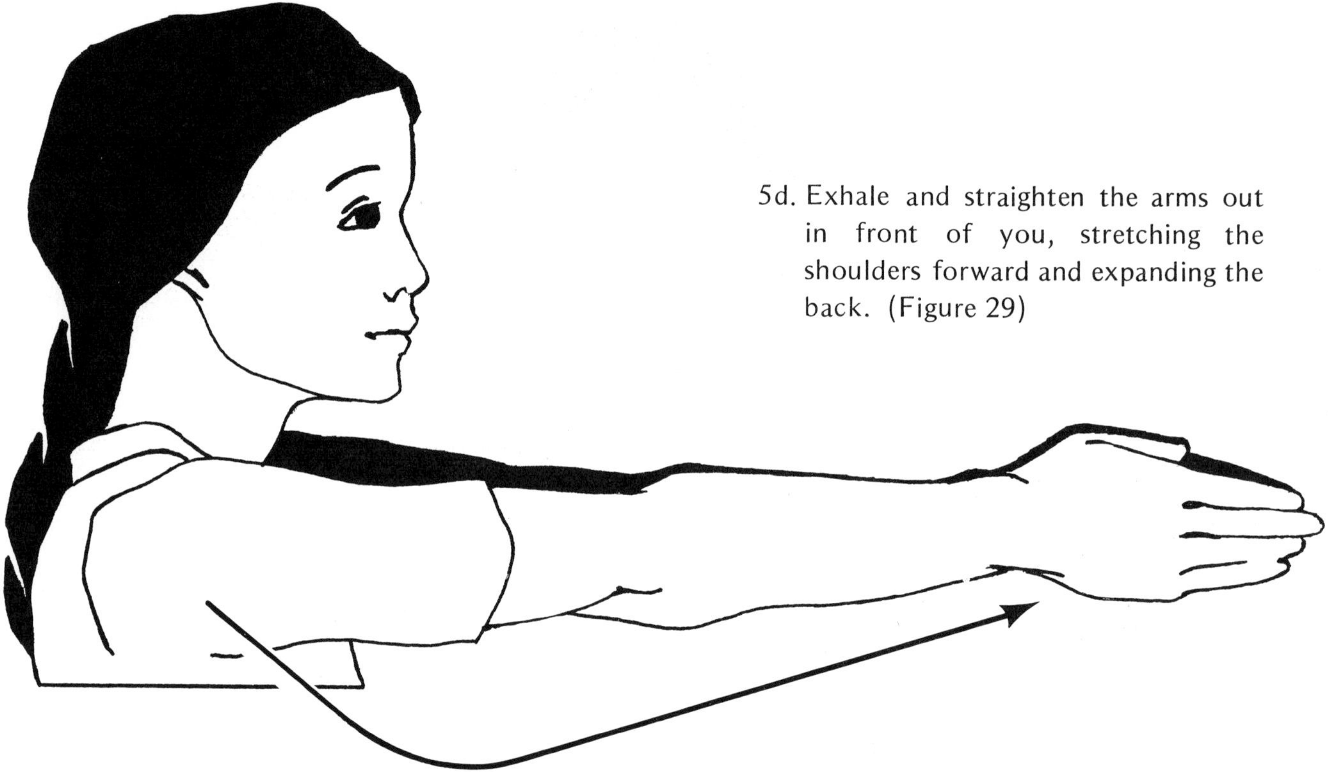

5d. Exhale and straighten the arms out in front of you, stretching the shoulders forward and expanding the back. (Figure 29)

Figure 29

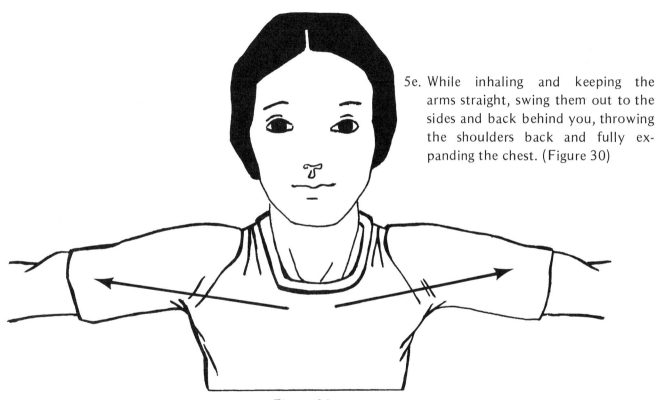

5e. While inhaling and keeping the arms straight, swing them out to the sides and back behind you, throwing the shoulders back and fully expanding the chest. (Figure 30)

Figure 30

Figure 31

SHOULDER WINGS

6. Bend the arms and place the fingers on the shoulders. (Figure 31) Begin to rotate the arms from the shoulders, stretching the elbows out to the front, bringing them together, expanding the back. Raise the elbows up high and then back, bringing the shoulder-blades close together and expanding the chest. Lower the elbows and without stopping, continue the rotation. Stretch and rotate several times in this direction and then reverse and go an equal number of times in the opposite direction.

ARMS, HANDS AND WRISTS

1. Stretch the arms out in front of you with the palms down and the arms level with the shoulders. Hold the arms straight without movement. Keep the fingers straight. Bending at the wrists, stretch the hands upward until the fingers point towards the ceiling and the back of the hands face you. (Figure 32) Return to the center and repeat twice.

Figure 32

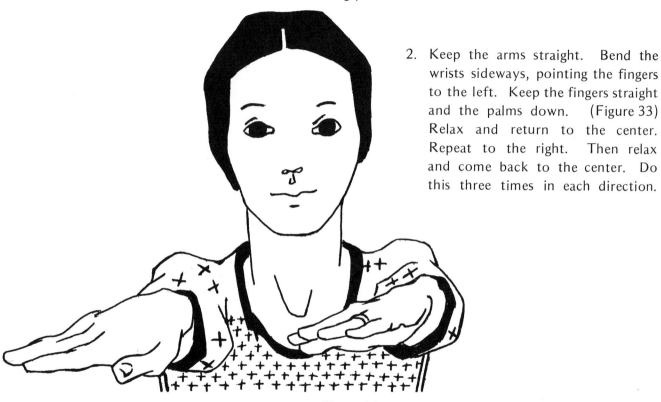

2. Keep the arms straight. Bend the wrists sideways, pointing the fingers to the left. Keep the fingers straight and the palms down. (Figure 33) Relax and return to the center. Repeat to the right. Then relax and come back to the center. Do this three times in each direction.

Figure 33

3.   Rotate the hands at the wrists, the left hand in a clockwise direction and the right hand in a counter-clockwise direction. Keep the arms straight and do not allow the forearms to move.   Reverse and rotate the same number of times in the opposite direction.

4.   Rotate both hands together in a clockwise direction, and then in a counter-clockwise direction.   Rotate the hands three times in each direction.

5.   Rotate the hands in the same way with spread fingers.

6.   Rotate the hands with claw fingers.

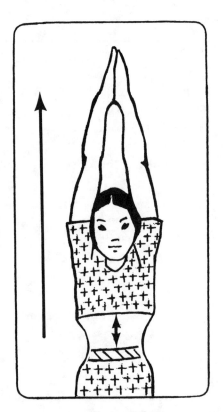

Figure 34

ABDOMEN AND TORSO

OVERHEAD STRETCH

1. Stand erect, feet firmly on the floor. Inhaling, stretch the arms straight above the head and place the palms together as in prayer form. Without lifting the heels, stretch up towards the ceiling as high as you can, stretching the whole body. Press the palms together and the upper arms against the ears. Feel as though you are lifting the trunk off the pelvis. (Figure 34) Exhaling, relax the arms completely and let them drop to the sides.

SIDEWAYS STRETCH

2. Stand firm and bring the arms straight up to the sides, level with the shoulders. Inhale, stretch as though trying to touch the two walls, stretching the arms out to the sides as far as possible. Feel as though you're stretching the elbows, wrists, and finally reach out with the fingers. With an exhalation, bring the arms back down to the sides and relax. (Figure 35)

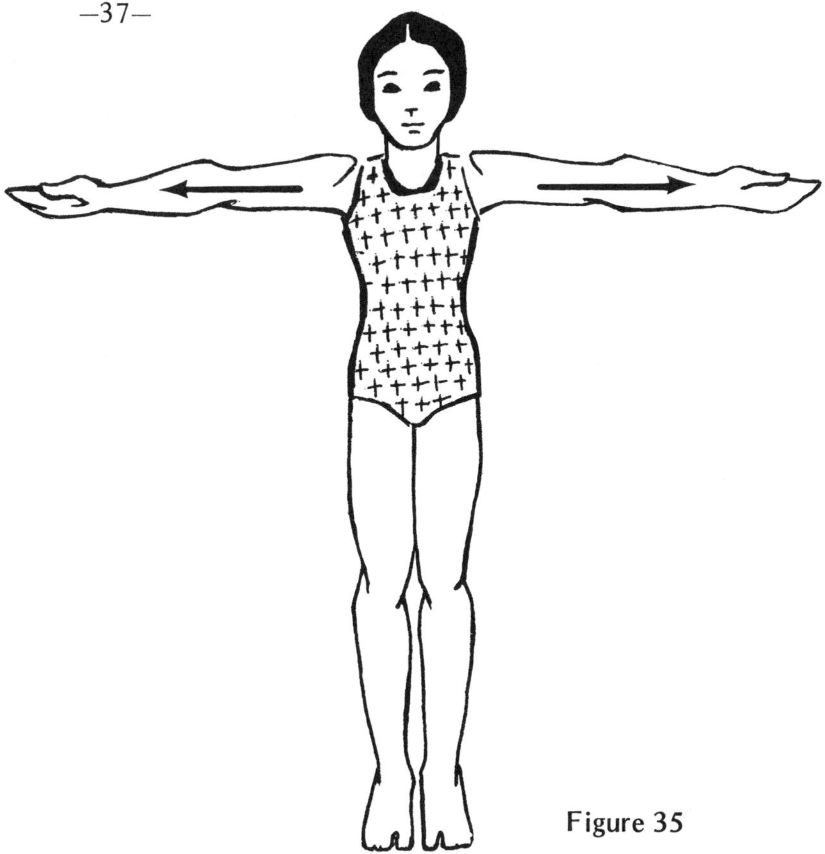

Figure 35

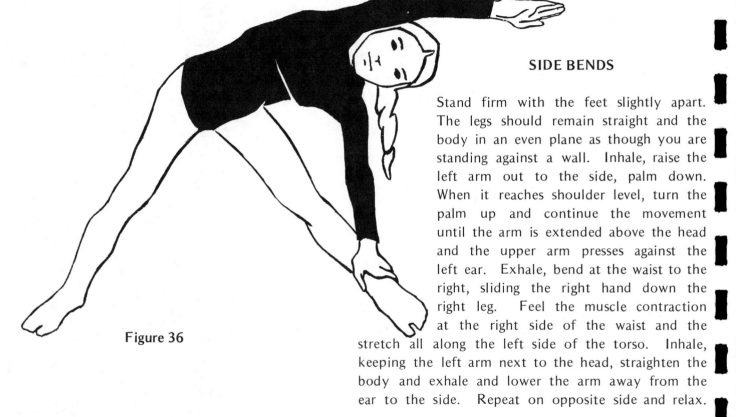

Figure 36

SIDE BENDS

Stand firm with the feet slightly apart. The legs should remain straight and the body in an even plane as though you are standing against a wall. Inhale, raise the left arm out to the side, palm down. When it reaches shoulder level, turn the palm up and continue the movement until the arm is extended above the head and the upper arm presses against the left ear. Exhale, bend at the waist to the right, sliding the right hand down the right leg. Feel the muscle contraction at the right side of the waist and the stretch all along the left side of the torso. Inhale, keeping the left arm next to the head, straighten the body and exhale and lower the arm away from the ear to the side. Repeat on opposite side and relax.

TORSO TWIST

4a.   Stand erect with the feet two to three feet apart. Place the hands on the hips. Exhale and lean forward from the waist. According to your capacity, begin to rotate and twist making a complete circle, bending in all directions as far as you can. Rotate three times in each direction. Breathe evenly. It may be natural to exhale as you go forward and down and inhale as you raise up and bend back.

4b.   Stand erect with the feet two to three feet apart. Stretch the arms up and clasp the hands above the head. Exhale, and keeping the head between the arms, lean forward from the waist. Rotate and twist making a complete circle, three times in each direction as above.

4c.   Place hands on the hips. Exhale and lean forward from the hips. Then rotate as in the previous exercises.

4d.   Stretch the arms up and clasp the hands above the head. Exhale, keeping the head between the arms, lean forward from the hips. Rotate and twist as in the other exercises.

Figure 37

TAKING IN AND OUT OF STOMACH
(Akunchana Prasarana)

Sit on heels, bending forward with hands on the knees. With exhalation force the stomach up and in; with inhalation, let it fall passively. Repeat this as many times as is comfortable. (Figure 37)

Figure 38

ABDOMINAL LIFT *(Uddiyana Bandha)*

Stand with feet about two feet apart. Keeping the spine straight, bend the knees slightly and lean forward from the waist just far enough to place the palms of the hands squarely on the thighs just above the knees. Let the weight of the torso be down the arms. Suck the diaphragm in and up, keeping the air out. Pull the navel towards the spine and the diaphragm up behind the rib cage creating a civity there. (Figure 38) Hold for as long as you comfortably can, retaining the breath out. Slowly inhale and relax according to your capacity. (See section on the therapeutic value of *asanas*.) This exercise should not be done if any of the following conditions are present: high blood pressure, ulcers, and heart disorders. Women should not perform this exercise during the menstrual cycle or during pregnancy.

TORSO AND LEGS

STANDING FORWARD BEND

Stand firm with the feet spread well apart. Inhale and raise the arms over the head with the palms facing forward. With an exhalation, begin to bend forward, moving the arms and shoulders imitating a swimming motion. The motion of the arms and the forward bending movement, alternatively stretch first one side of the body and then the other. Make the movements smooth and rhythmic. Inhaling slowly, raise up, continuing the same motion. Stand erect, lower the arms and relax. This exercise is a preparation for the forward bending *asanas*. It loosens the thigh joints and stretches the muscles of the back of the legs and the back.

TWISTING BEND

Stand with the feet two to three feet apart. Inhaling, raise the arms straight out to the sides level with the shoulders. With an exhalation, bend forward and, twisting the trunk, touch the right hand to the left foot and turn the head and look up at the up-raised left hand. Twist to the right touching the left hand to the right foot and turning the head to look at the right hand now high in the air. Alternate on this twisting from side to side according to your capacity.

LEGS AND FEET

LEG KICK

Stand firm and place the hands on the waist. Lift the left foot off the floor and bring it forward slightly, finding your balance on the right foot. Keep both legs straight. With a sharp movement, kick the leg back to touch the buttocks with the heel. Let the leg return to the starting position (slightly lifted from the floor). Repeat with the right leg.

KNEE SWIRL

With the same stance as above, raise the left knee and let the leg from the knee and down hang loosely. Begin to gently swing the leg at the knee in a circular motion. First clockwise, then counter-clockwise, trying not to move the thigh. The calf, ankle and foot should remain relaxed throughout the rotation. Relax and repeat with the right leg.

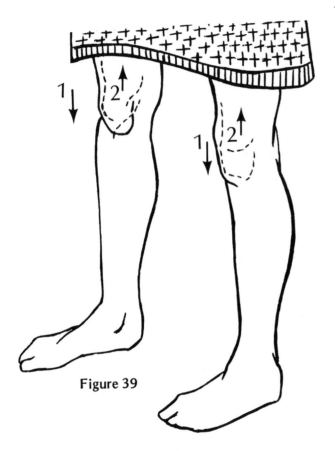

Figure 39

DANCING KNEES

Stand with the feet spread slightly. Tense and lift all the muscles of the thigh and around the left knee cap, raising the knee cap. (Figure 39) Relax and let it fall back into place. Alternate left and right knees.

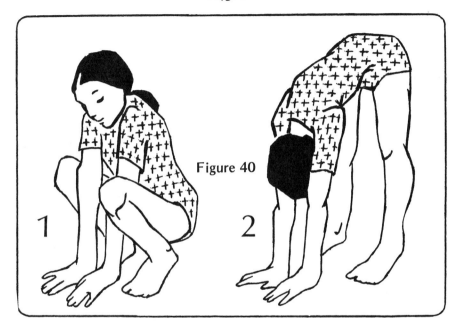

Figure 40

KNEE BENDS

Spread the feet about a foot apart and , keeping the feet flat on the floor, squat down with the buttocks near the fllor. Rest the hands on the floor in front of you. (Figure 40, no. 1) Inhale and raise the hips up, straightening the legs, but let the hands remain on the floor or close to the floor. (Figure 40, no. 2) Then exhale and squat again between the knees. Repeat several times.

Figure 41

ANKLE SQUAT

Spread the feet about a foot apart and keeping the feet flat on the floor, squat down with the buttock near the floor. Become balanced in this position. The arms can rest over the knees or can come forward slightly and rest with the back of the upper arms against the shins. (Figure 41) Remain in this position for up to one minute.

ANKLE & FEET

1. Stand erect with the hands on the waist. Keep the left leg straight and lift it six inches off the floor. Bending at the ankle, lift the foot up, pointing the toes toward the ceiling. Relax the foot. Then point the toes downward as far as possible, then relax it.

2. Without turning or twisting the leg, turn the foot and ankle to the left, pointing the toes as far out to the side as possible (Figure 42) Return to center. Turn the foot in, pointing the toes towards the right. Bring it back to center position.

3. Rotate the foot (only the ankle and foot should move) first to the left, then up to the right, and down, touching on the four points mentioned above. Rotate three times in each direction.

4. Bring the foot back to the floor. Relax completely in a standing position, then repeat the exact movements with the right foot.

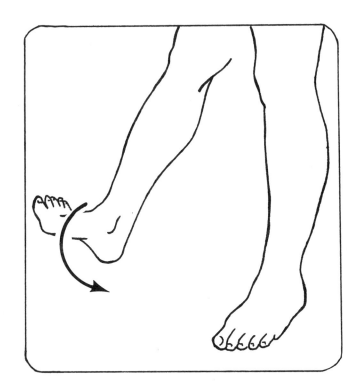

Figure 42

TOE BALANCE

1. Stand straight with the feet together and the hands on the hips. Inhale and raise up onto the toes. (Figure 43) When the inhalation is complete, exhale and lower the heels back to the floor. Repeat several times.

2. Raise up onto the toes as indicated above and hold up to thirty seconds or to your capacity. It helps the balance if the gaze is fixed on an object. After becoming steady in this position, perform the same with the eyes closed.

3. Stand erect with the feet close together. Inhale and simultaneously raise up onto the toes and raise the arms straight out in front of you level with the shoulder with the palms turned down. (Figure 43)

4. Keeping the trunk, arms and head stationary, exhale and turn to the left as far as you can, twisting from the waist and continuing to balance on the toes. (Figure 43) Inhale and come back to the center, then turn to the right in the same manner. After proper balance is achieved, perform the above movements with the eyes closed.

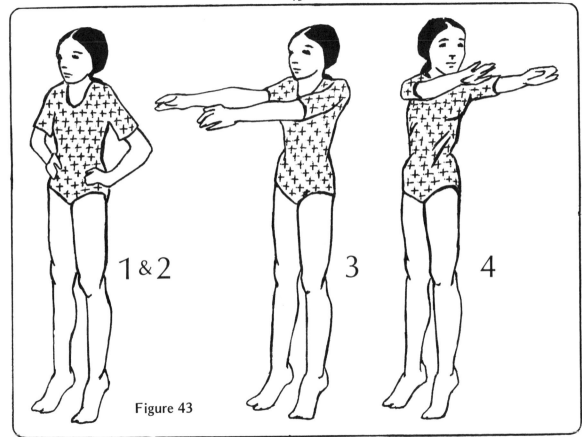

1 & 2

3

4

Figure 43

BOOKS PUBLISHED BY THE HIMALAYAN INSTITUTE